Naughty Coupons for Boyfriend

dress up night- you pick the outfit

lmfao, that made me laugh

blumpkin (blowjob while taking a shit)

spur of the moment 69 followed by anal

strap me to bed and ride me

naughty lingerie night

just something that you guys
don't normally do,
but something that you know
he would be into

night out at a strip club
and you both get lap dances

pegging (if he's interested)

fantasy night
(in which you'd fulfill one of your partner's)

purchase of one toy of his/her choice

position of his/her choice

make dessert of your partner –
whipped cream, chocolate, cherries, etc.

fantasy play and naked housework is always good

sexy photo shoot
(if you'd be comfortable with that)

spontanious, random make-
outage/sex at the cardholder's whim

anywhere-but-the-bedroom night

mandantory go to a movie
and make out the whole time night

what to wear free pass

do what you want with Ice

whip cream / chocolate syrup

lingerie treat modeled

sensual massage followed by blowjob to completion

any Position of choice

phone sex public place quicky

sex under the stars

licking of choice

bondage - handcuffed/blindfold

one toy of choice

sensual vido rental of choice

he wishes to do

personal slave service/servan

spanking you/you being his sex slave for an hour

giving him a blowjob while he is watching porn

sex in public place

serve my favorite meal to me naked

79130929R00057

Made in the USA
Middletown, DE
07 July 2018